Walking on the Moon

Ry Reed

Ry Reed Books

Thank you so much for purchasing this book! Don't forget to leave a review. I want you to share your thoughts with the world.

Thank you!

Books by Ry Reed

Poetry

PINK GRAPEFRUIT

WHITE ORCHIDS

GREY STORM CLOUDS

THE LITTLE RED POETRY BOOK CALLED HEARTBREAK

WALKING ON THE MOON

A WELL OF THOUGHTS

I love classic love songs. Bobby Caldwell's "What You Won't Do for Love," Delegation's "Oh Honey," Mint Condition's "Breakin' My Heart (Pretty Brown Eyes)," Maxwell's "Pretty Wings." I love how we play these songs at weddings, proms, birthday parties, and family reunions. Basically, on special occasions, you'll always find a couple swaying on the dance floor, reminiscing, remembering the exact song they fell in love with. I love how these songs are our go-to romantic hits. That's when it hit me; I would write a poetry book like a classic love song, something you'd play (read) when you wanted to remember how good it feels to be in love. You send the song (book) to the love of your life when you're thinking of them. A cute wake-up reminder to let them know they're on your mind. I wanted poems that were useable and sendable, and endearing. So use my poems like that, shareable messages to the ones you love. Send them to anyone on your mind. Send them to someone you hope will fall in love with you. Send them to the love of your life. Send them to people in passing. Create smiles and laughter. Read them for you and everyone else. But give my poems away. It's all I ask.

I hope my poems reach everyone you love,

Cheers.

Fall in love with someone who pours into your cup so your love continuously overflows like waterfalls filling blue oceans. This is how it should be.

-Ry Reed

CONTENTS

Books by Ry Reed	**4**
CONTENTS	**7**
Cloud coverings	24
Restless appetite	26
So I learned	27
Sweet and bitter	28
Whole wheat	29
Limit breaker	30
What's hanging around you	31
Needed me	32
My best line	33
Where you left it	34
Want what you want	35
End of your world	36
It didn't matter	37
Fit together	38
Waiting for you	39
Open the window	40
Peaches	41
Back to sea	42

Glue back together	43
Difficult for you	44
A thousand miles	45
The only thing	46
Our first kiss	47
Stars aligned	48
Hurt me	49
Didn't need much	50
Not the one	51
The little things	52
Shape of your heart	53
Diving	54
Move forward	55
Heal all wounds	56
Learned how to fly	57
Your smile	58
Internal	59
Find peace	60
Wild daises	61
Lost in their storm	62
Keep you warm	63
Your song	64
Blue moons	65

Ocean's sand	66
Let's play UNO	67
Lost in the clouds	68
hug me	69
Promise me	70
Together we can	71
Forgive me	73
Quietly waiting	74
Adoring stars	75
Best place	76
My arms	77
Love all of you	78
Soul touch	79
Long day	80
Rarely come	81
Half your heart	82
Missing you	83
Home on earth	84
Giver her everything	85
Powerful lessons	86
A cold piece	87
She might leave	88
I wonder	89

Back home	90
Stung	91
Forced forward	92
Lose count	93
Our breaths	94
Stared too deeply	95
Small victories	96
Adoring words	97
To the moon	98
Umbrellas	99
Made for you	100
Hersey kisses	101
Shatter	102
Flu season pickup line	103
See ya later	104
The deep blue	105
I'm listening	106
We haven't talked in a while	107
Palm lines	108
Come or go	109
Her favorite flowers	110
Give her space to gather herself	111
There was us	112

Tap water	113
Laughing too hard	114
Rearrange	115
I'm here now	116
Excited to meet you	117
Every season	118
Two lungs	119
Is elbow kissing okay?	120
No expectations required	121
Something nice for her	122
A thought to think	123
Past trauma stings	124
Close and personal	125
Water her daily	126
Madly in love	127
Good can become evil	128
Carbon and hydrogen	129
The last drop	130
Your hand wants mine	131
Functioning addict	132
All of your soul	133
Confident lover	134
Waves	135

If you leave her	136
What colors shall I paint with?	137
Our silence	139
Field of lilies	140
Snares and nets	141
Talks in private	142
Leads to you	143
Ask her questions	144
Hold her	145
Thinking of you	146
Follow through	147
When she's falling apart	148
Easily taken back	149
Tell me what you like	150
Drugs then you	151
Coat pockets	152
Open more up	153
Fly away	154
Some sugar	155
If you were…	156
Tornado	157
Guarded hearts	158
Eye for an eye	159

She moved on	160
Crazy	161
Burning building	162
Not yet	163
Everything I need	164
Understanding her	165
Every moment	166
Conversations over the phone	167
No cages	168
Your two hands	169
Epic storm	170
A little you	171
How have you been?	172
Little broken pieces	173
Let them come	174
Enamored	175
Hello soul	176
I'm a clown	177
We	178
Mysterious stranger	179
I hope	180
Lazy hours	181
Endless well	182

Things we shared	183
You're a mood	184
Wild butterflies	185
Go see the world	186
Rainy days	187
Together and apart	188
Don't forget this	189
I shouldn't have	190
Messed up	191
Chipped watches	192
Fake things and mean faces	193
Pillows and feathers	194
To the bitter end	195
Your words	196
Sugar fiend	197
In the meantime	198
Your flaws	199
She's loved you	200
Dracula's fangs	201
Teenage fantasy	202
Here you go	203
Bride of Frankenstein	204
All that matters	205

Trust fall	206
Careful love	207
It's never too late	208
A bad hand	209
Old days	210
Tight	211
Chase after you	212
What will you give	213
They already left	214
Ruined	215
Felt	216
Hurt me hurt you	217
Really real	218
Traps	219
The real you	220
Cuddles	221
We've all done it	222
To the sun	223
Have you heard this song?	224
Future vision	225
Rare	226
Miss me	227
Here to stay	228

Controlling	229
Hands	230
Small hugs	231
Unimportant	232
She is	233
Romance	234
Time infinity	235
Dreaming of you	236
Eating alone	237
Showing up	238
Home struck	239
Close to me	240
Pouring	241
End	242
Need you	243
Very sweet	244
Together	245
Earth to mars	246
Red wine	247
Sunflower seeds	248
Wild child	249
She wants you	250
I'm cutting onions that's why I'm crying	251

Stand-by	252
Actions	253
Home sweet home	254
Gravity	255
Her interest	256
Smile more	257
Possession	258
Longing	259
Pillows and blankets	260
Glass slipper	261
Let it hurt	262
Please and thank you	263
Birthright	264
Knock first	265
A lifetime of regrets	266
It's a little cold	267
Tell me	268
Outer shell	269
Photography	270
Deep slumber	271
It takes two to build a house	272
I'll wait here	273
Where have you been?	274

Let me have some	275
Overwatering	276
Tug of war	277
You're in	278
Connected	279
If you leave, it's okay	280
I miss you	281
Back to bed	282
Eyes	283
I'll be bored	284
Up all night	285
My name is	286
Ebb and flow	288
Lazy painter	289
Mood swings	290
One more	291
Eight hours later	292
Too much in common	293
Can I see you later?	294
Her emotions are clever	295
To speak	296
You go first	297
You're so beautiful	298

Some advice	299
Porch lights on	300
Lifetime warranty	301
Ideal body	302
I'm listening	303
Lock the door	305
Stays in	306
Deep breaths	307
Go slow	308
Grows slowly	309
No comparison	310
Statue of David	311
Not just a smile	312
Lost looking at you	313
Drowning	314
Two more hours	315
Mending heart	316
Skeptical lover	317
Bad days	318
Looks with both eyes	320
Giving energy	321
Read this again	322
Overthinking the uncomplicated	323

She looks for the best	324
Treat her kindly	325
Petty tings	326
What did you just say?	327
Treasure chest	328
I'll be over here	330
What are you fighting for again?	331
Too immature	332
What's really going on?	333
Star crossed lovers	334
Intentional bump	335
Tell her what you want	336
Leave the party	337
We haven't gone deep yet	338
Her emotions tell her everything	339
Beast's rose	341
She's that good	342
She thought this through	343
Miles away	344
Rare diamonds	346
Feel it in my soul	347
Give her what she wants	348
A thousand storms	349

Homebound	350
The kiss of death	351
Listen first	352
Mistakes	353
A phone call away	354
Tell me everything	355
Shovel and pail	356
Swept off feet	357
Trust fall	358
Too dangerous	359
Be very afraid of her	360
Out of body	361
Come close	362
Crash	363
Tell me your story	364
A kind and balanced relationship	365
I love all of you and everything in between	366
So you're addicted to avocados?	368
You can	369
Neighboring stars	370
Inner mirror	371
Treat her kindly	372
She has two sides	373

Build this home with your hands	374
Trojan horse	375
Fly with support	376
Watering	377
Above	378
Nighttime poem	379
Wishbone	381
Smile for me	382
Fresh scars	383
Shattered plates	384
Sensitive souls	385
Scabs	386
Disconnection	387
Another one, please	388
Kind words	389
A born lover	390
Fire walker	391
Bloody knees	392
She can fly	393
I'm the s**t	394
Remain cool	395
That's a threat	396
Fought my hardest	397

About the author	**399**
Latest Releases	401
Ry Reed's social media	**405**

I thought it would be brighter without your light

Guiding me in the dark,

But why would clouds want to live

Without the moon's luminous glow?

Cloud coverings

The worst pains are the ones we allow to happen over and over again.

Repeated injuries

My arms will forever crave you…

Restless appetite

I gave it my all, and my all wasn't what you were looking for…

So I learned

We were sweeter than iced tea on a hot day in June,

And we were bitter like cold coffee on a rainy day

In December.

Sweet and bitter

When I randomly thought of you in the bread aisle at 4:43 p.m., I knew it was love.

Whole wheat

We come to discover our limits after they've been broken…

Limit breaker

You attract what you allow to stay…

What's hanging around you

It's the little things I miss

Like how you looked at me

When no one was around.

And it's the little things

I won't miss like how you

Chose not to look at me

When I needed you.

Needed me

We fit together like peanut butter and jelly…that's all I got.

My best line

My heart is where you left it…on unread

Where you left it

You were everything I thought I was looking for and everything I didn't need. But I still wanted you.

Want what you want

Heartbreaks aren't the end of the world. It just feels like it when the world you made together falls apart.

End of your world

I should have told you how I felt.

But after you told me how you felt,

It didn't matter anymore.

It didn't matter

The way our hands fit together was what I looked forward to the most.

Fit together

When the sun fades away,

Stealing earth away with it,

You find out how not alone you are.

The moon is waiting for you.

Waiting for you

Your reflection won't show how you feel inside.
Only windows can do that.

Open the window

Your lips are sweet like peaches.

Peaches

Lost at sea can be mesmerizing.

You forget what land looks like and choose to sail on ocean waves under a clear blue sky. You feel more welcomed the longer you stay afloat. It's not until the ship sinks and you're gasping for air that you realize how crazy you were for leaving land. But we return to the sea because it draws us out of our comfort zone, and we like the rush.

Back to sea

When you've glued your heart back together, you learn not to give it away to any and everybody ever again.

Glue back together

People interested in you won't make it difficult for you to spend time with them. They won't play games, they won't change their mind at the last minute, no cancellations and work delays will stop them from seeing you. You've been on their mind all day. They're excited to see you and hope you're excited to see them too. They want to spend time with you.

Difficult for you

I've walked a thousand miles for you and will walk
a thousand more to be with you.

A thousand miles

My heart beats slower the farther you move away from me. It's because you're the only thing that makes my heart beat.

The only thing

I knew I was addicted after our first kiss.

Our first kiss

Talking at night under the night sky did something to your chemistry and mine. Our stars aligned.

Stars aligned

If you love me, then why did you hurt me?

You hurt me because you stopped

Considering me and

Did what you wanted to do the most.

Hurt me

I didn't need much,

Just love and loyalty.

The little I needed,

You never gave.

Didn't need much

If you have to consider loving me

Then I'm not the one

Because if I was the one

I would be your only option

Not the one

The little things you thought were unimportant

Were important to me

Like how the small dimple on your right cheek

Appears when you laugh

The little things

I knew the shape of your heart like how you knew the shape of my lips…

Shape of your heart

We fear diving if we don't think we'll be able to come back up for air. But I was all the air you would have ever needed if you trusted me.

Diving

Walking away is neither fun nor easy,

But you keep walking because

Life moves you forward.

Move forward

Time does heal all wounds…

If you're strong enough and

Don't reopen them.

Heal all wounds

When you learned how to fly

I thought you would one day

Fly back home to me.

Learned how to fly

It began with your smile.

It led to a laugh.

It ended with a hug.

Your smile

Hearts do bleed,

Internally

Where no one can see

Internal

Find your peace of mind when you determine what gives you peace

Find peace

Whenever I smell wild daisies,
I think of you.

Wild daises

There are people like this:

When they are hurting, they push you away so you can't feel or see them. They close themselves off from the world and you. They bind their love from ever loving you. These people love the hardest and have a hard time loving when lost in their storms.

Lost in their storm

I'll keep your hands warm when it's cold. That's what my jacket is made for.

Keep you warm

Not everyone wants to dance to your song.

That's okay.

Keep dancing anyway.

Your song

Blue moons fall

On the lines of your

Back and mine,

Cool air creeps

Between cheek to cheek.

The hush of your sleepy breath

Soothes my thoughts

To ease.

I trace your brow

In the moonlight

Blue moons

We like to lay on

Ocean's sand because

It warms up all the

Frozen parts of us

We've kept cold.

Ocean's sand

Love doesn't have to be like chess.

Love should feel like UNO.

Everyone gets a turn.

A reverse to through you off.

You retaliate with a plus two

Or four.

You play fair,

And at the end,

After all the jokes and laughter,

You want to play

Again and again.

Let's play UNO

I had been lost in the clouds

For so long

It was hard coming back down

To earth

Without you…

Lost in the clouds

Hug me like we're long lost lovers

hug me

I'll be your oxygen

If you promise to be my gravity…

Promise me

Together

We can climb the tallest mountains,

Together

We can form planets

And plant stars,

Together

We can soak up oceans

And dance for rain,

Together

We can be everything,

Anything,

And all the little things we love in between

Together we can

Sorry I missed your call,

I was busy texting you…

Before I hurt you,

I'm sorry…

Forgive me

Find me quietly waiting for your love.

Quietly waiting

If you're a star,

Then I will be an astronomer

Adoring you from afar.

Adoring stars

The best place to heal is within yourself.

Best place

The safest place to rest is in my arms.

My arms will hold you

When you're tired.

My arms

I love all the little weird things about you.

Love all of you

When you touched my hand,
You touched my soul.

Soul touch

She can appear strong on the outside,

Work hard,

Manage her business,

Life,

Be there for her friends when they need her,

Mentor,

Fight battles that leave her bloody and blue,

But when she comes home to you

She's hoping you'll be there

To help her clean all her wounds and

Polish her sword

After a long day gone.

Long day

They'll look back and appreciate everything you did once you're gone. Loving, caring, generous people like you rarely come around.

Rarely come

People don't realize what they have until they get with someone with half the heart and love you had. It's an eye awakening experience.

Half your heart

If you were good to them, they will miss you.

Missing you

Find me floating on the dark side of the moon

Gliding between your comets

Avoiding your meteor showers

I live to see you fall

A wanderer of lifeless seas

Missing air

I'll wait to feel your gravity

Back home on earth.

Home on earth

To give your all…

Is all she asked for.

Giver her everything

There are no regrets,

Only powerful lessons.

Powerful lessons

Her silence will be excruciating.

You might be stuck on all the warm

And heartfelt things she did

And once was.

It'll hurt because

She won't want to do those things for you

Anymore.

Her coldness will bother you for years.

A cold piece

If you take her for granted,

There's a strong possibility

She might

Get tired and walk away.

She might leave

I love how much you wonder if I'm thinking about you…

I wonder

If you ever get lost,

I'll find a way to guide you back home.

Back home

I was a bee

And you were my victim

Stung

I died

Needing to be close to you…

Stung

You told her to go,

And she walked away

Dragging her feet

Forcing her heart

To go onward

Forced forward

I continuously lose count

Of all the ribs

Encasing your heart.

Lose count

When we breathed

I felt every inch of air filling my lungs…

Our breaths

Have you ever stared so intensely into someone's eyes and lost yourself looking too deeply into the depths of their soul? You forget how to think and move. Time is irrelevant. All other worldly matters don't matter.

Stared too deeply

Your smile wasn't just a smile to me.

Your smile was a micro victory

I thanked heaven for.

Small victories

The only language I want to speak is I love you…

Adoring words

I'll follow your footsteps to the moon.

To the moon

If it rained,

I would find a way

To keep you dry.

Umbrellas

My hand was made to hold yours...

Made for you

Hey,

Do you want to know what

The sweetest thing on the planet is?

A kiss from you.

Hersey kisses

Hold her

She is glass.

If you drop her

She shatters.

Shatter

Corny pickup line:

(pretend to sneeze)

"I'm sorry. I've been feeling under the weather without you to keep me warm."

Flu season pickup line

When people walk away,
Let them go.

See ya later

Choosing to love you means

That I adore your soul.

I'm able to look beyond your surface

And have fallen in love

With all your shades of blue.

The deep blue

The best way to reach her heart is by listening.

I'm listening

Take a step back. Ask her questions. See what's on her mind. Not a lot of people do this.

We haven't talked in a while

The lines on your palms

Is secretly a map

To your heart

I will spend eternity

Trying to decipher

Palm lines

Love in such a way that they are free to stay,
And free to go.

Come or go

Might be cliché

But

You'll make her smile

If you give her flowers.

Not any ordinary flowers,

Her favorite flowers,

Bundled together.

Give them to her on a

Not so special occasion.

Her favorite flowers

If she ever backs away when something is on her mind, that means she's not ready to talk to you about her problems. There is love in space. When she's ready to talk, you'll be the first person she wants to talk to. You'll push her further away if you rush her into opening up.

Give her space to gather herself

At night,

There were stars

There were candles

And,

There was us

There was us

I would learn how to dance on water

If it meant dancing with you…

Tap water

I like the way you laugh

So hard

Into me

That you

Stop breathing.

That makes me

Laugh.

Laughing too hard

Can I trade u and I for us?

Rearrange

Well, you are special.

I don't care what

Anyone before me

Said…

I'm here now

Is it déjà vu

Or

Have I dreamed

Of meeting you

Before?

Excited to meet you

I fell in love with you in spring,

We spent lazy nights together in summer,

We drank spiced lattes on picnics in fall,

You kept me warm in winter.

Every season

How we learned how to breathe together will always fascinate me.

Two lungs

Have you ever kissed someone's elbow?

Haha I don't know if you're

Supposed to?

Is elbow kissing okay?

Compliment her without expecting anything.

No expectations required

Sometimes, but not all the time, surprise her with her favorite drink. Don't ask her beforehand. Don't give her any clues that you're doing something nice for her. Just do something nice.

Something nice for her

Isn't it strange how we find the courage to confess our feelings at night, or do we feel so vulnerable at night that we would rather show ourselves when it's harder to be seen?

A thought to think

If you push her away…

She'll remember how being

Pushed away felt.

A little wall will form around her heart.

She'll never let herself feel

That way again.

Past trauma stings

Beauty is better seen up close and personal.

Close and personal

Water her love daily

Lease she dies…

Water her daily

Was it candy,

Or the sinister taste of her lips

That drove you mad?

Madly in love

She can either melt in your arms or fly away without a single feather missing. She'll yearn for you like how fire begs for wood and how a honeybee searches for pollen, or she will be like the monster from the blue lagoon and drag you down to a watery grave.

Good can become evil

Don't expect her to be faithful

If you can't be loyal.

This is pure science.

Carbon and hydrogen

Kiss me

Like you're dying of thirst

And

I'm the only drop of water

For miles…

The last drop

It's so interesting how your hand and my hand want to be close when we're together. My hand can't stop trying to trace your hand, and your hand can't stop trying to bring my hand to your heart.

Your hand wants mine

I can be a functioning drug addict.

As long as you kiss me once a day

For my daily high…

Functioning addict

I love you because I accept all of you.

All of your imperfections,

All of your habits,

The way you process information

And see the world.

I love your every blemish,

Every scar,

Every wound.

It's your soul I cannot live without.

All of your soul

Be a confident lover.

When they come

Adore them.

When they go

Respect them.

If they come back

Appreciate them.

If they never come back,

Remember them.

But let them go freely

And lovingly.

Confident lover

Leave me lost at sea

If it means that

I'm one wave closer to finding you…

Waves

If you leave her,

She'll give you all the space you really didn't want.

If you leave her

Tell me what color to paint the sky.

I'll paint all your dreams

Even if it takes all my life.

What colors shall I paint with?

It's fair to say that

You confused the living hell out of me

Because you barely made any sense

And that's why I couldn't leave you,

Now I don't make any sense.

Makes no sense

To be so comfortable in our silence gave me peace.

Our silence

Find me scattered across a field of lilies

When you rise in the east

I call dew to awaken me

I pray your light falls warmly

On my petals and leaves

How will I ever survive

Without you?

Darkness would take me

Too soon.

Stay with me

Let tonight come

Later than sooner

My love.

Let our afternoons be lazy and long

Tangled in grass

Field of lilies

I caught you

In a net

Capable of snaring the most

Daring

Wild

Ravenous creatures

This world has ever seen.

I lured you in with

A promise

And a kiss.

You haven't escaped.

Not once.

Snares and nets

If you're quiet long enough,

You'll hear all the little things

She wants you to know about her.

She'll tell you them once.

That's how she is.

A mysterious soul,

An aloof woman,

A silent spirit,

A set mold.

Listen,

She speaks her mind in private.

Talks in private

There's nowhere I can go

Where a compass

Won't lead me to you…

Leads to you

She loves it when you ask her questions about her. She has so many stories to share. She's waiting for the perfect person to share them with.

Ask her questions

Hold her in your arms like you're her blanket

And without you

She'll freeze.

Hold her

I don't skip, but my heart skips a beat when I think of you...

Thinking of you

A sexy trait: when you do what you say you're going to do.

Follow through

Pull her close when she feels like she's falling apart. Your arms will be the glue that holds her together.

When she's falling apart

When you easily take back someone who mistreats you, your actions tell them three things: that they can get away with anything, you'll keep taking them back, and you don't value yourself because you tolerate their behavior.

Easily taken back

I won't know how to love you unless you tell me what you like and don't like. You'll be unhappy if you play nice and sweep everything you don't like underneath the rug. Hiding your true feelings causes more damage than good because not expressing your problems only works until you explode.

Tell me what you like

There are drugs,

Then there's you…

Drugs then you

The only way to warm up

Cold hands

Is by stuffing them

Into your coat pockets…

Coat pockets

Remember,

She can't read your mind.

She doesn't always know what's going on in there.

If you don't open up,

She'll start fabricating

Conclusions

Before you have a chance to

Clear your name.

Open more up

If you fly away,

I'll be where you left me…

Minding my own damn business.

Fly away

These are the ingredients

Needed to make pink lemonade:

Water, lemons, blush, and give me some sugar.

Some sugar

If you were a star,

I would wish for you.

If you were a tree,

I would pick you for shade.

If you were a witch,

I would want your curse.

If you were a bee,

I would let you turn me into honey.

If you were...

The only difference between you and a tornado is that you blew me away, and the tornado didn't.

Tornado

I won't be easy to understand

I'm telling you this so you'll know

Frustration is a word that will come to your mind

This, I'm sure.

We aren't foes

But I treat you as such.

Be patient with me.

My version of love is rough because

I'm familiar with bleeding

But if you stick around

Longer than the last one

I'll show you the most important thing

I guard to death

Living inside of me.

Guarded hearts

She'll burn you if you cut her.

Eye for an eye

If she moved on,

That means she's had enough. She's at her breaking point and doesn't have the strength to pick up the pieces and build again. She's tired. She's worn. She has accepted defeat. This is the end. If she suddenly ends things, her breaking point came a long time ago, and now, she found the courage to leave your ass.

She moved on

It drives me crazy

How much attention

Your neck needs.

Crazy

What you thought was a safe place

To rest your head

Was actually a building

Set to catch on fire.

You came perfect

But imperfect timing

Was inescapable.

They set everything on fire.

Burning building

She only brings up the past because she's not over it yet…

Not yet

There's a blanket, a pillow, soft music, warm coffee, rain, and you.

Everything I need

She'll back the hell up from you if you move too fast. If you keep pushing, she'll ignore you. If you give her space and time to understand her feelings for you, she'll start falling in love with you. If you stay away after she falls in love with you, she will go insane trying to find you.

Understanding her

She has complex emotions swirling inside her that she doesn't always understand. Her moods change with her feelings. Confusing, but she feels what she feels in the moment. If she loves you, she loves you in that moment. To keep her loving you, consistently keep being what she needs in every moment.

Every moment

There's talking on the phone,
Then there's sharing your soul.

Conversations over the phone

Love,

But make sure they feel free.

No cages

Maybe heartbroken,

But not utterly destroyed.

You can rebuild again

With your two hands.

Your two hands

Love is like a boat in an epic storm,

If you two work together

You'll make it out.

If you fight,

Your boat will sink where it sits.

Epic storm

I don't need much to live.

A little water,

A little bread,

A little sunshine,

A little peace,

And a little you

To pass the time.

A little you

It wakes me

Always at the midnight hour.

Feelings of anxiety and wonderfully

Consuming curiosity.

A spell of spells

A maddening sickness ruined by my mind

Wondering

Thinking

Planning

Coordinating how I will build up the

Courage

To see how you're doing after so many years.

How have you been?

I can't love you without loving all the little broken pieces of your heart you unsuccessfully try to hide from me.

Little broken pieces

Once you put yourself out there

Let them freely come to you.

Don't force it.

Let them come willingly.

Don't forget that you're

The prize.

Let them come

If I stumble finding my words,

Know that I'm enamored by you.

Enamored

Stare too deeply into my eyes

You'll see a soul

Waiting to meet you

Hello soul

Were they eyes

Or the sky split in two?

Sneaky gazes

Mind running into mazes

Pretending to turn corners

Bumping into you.

Felt more like seas

Nervously brushing my knees

Less like butterflies

Mines were prickling bees.

You lookup

I look down.

I'm the clown

Who never got around

To jot your name down.

I'm a clown

We spoke with our lips,

We communicated with our hands…

We

A mysterious stranger will attract the world.

But too much dialog drives them away.

How unfair

But true.

Mysterious stranger

I hope I keep you up all night wondering about me.

I hope

All that mattered to me was
The lazy hours spent in your arms

Lazy hours

You are an endless well of knowledge.

How can I say

I know you

If I don't keep getting to know you?

Endless well

My hand became our hands

Your jacket became my blanket

My breakfast became your snack

Your plate became my appetizer

My bed became your sanctuary

Your sweats became my pajamas

My laptop became your tv

Your chains became my jewelry

My spot became our spot

We shared almost everything

Things we shared

There are moods,

But you're my nighttime high.

Best with deep thoughts,

My feelings swirl

Too deeply

Because everything you're saying

Is everything I'm liking.

Cool smooth R&B on shuffle

Like on cue

There are two views

You

And a starry moon

You're a mood

Thoughts of you

Cause butterflies

To run wild inside of me.

I let them

Run as wild as they want.

Wild butterflies

Roam free

See the world

See it like

Like how it's meant to be seen.

Every pond of water,

Forest so green,

Climb snowy cliffsides

Talk to people

On the oceanside.

When you remember me

And you will remember me

Imagine me talking to you

Beneath calm storms and yellow moons.

I stay casual.

I'm tethered to summer nights,

Cool autumns,

And selective moods.

Go see the world

She thinks better when it rains.

It soothes all her pains away.

Rainy days

When we're together

We start forest fires.

When we're apart,

I prefer sheltering in

Cold climates.

Together and apart

She deserves your very best. Not because it's the right thing to do but because this is how she should be treated. Always. There isn't a day that should go by where she's treated any less. If she is, you've forgotten how to treat a queen.

Don't forget this

I shouldn't have lied the same way you taught me to. Hiding how I felt seemed like the right thing to do to keep you a little bit longer than I needed to.

I shouldn't have

Messing up is one thing, but utterly destroying my heart could have been avoided…

Messed up

She's not broken.

A lot of s**t happened to her that

She has to live with.

She can love you,

But the last one did her

Wrong.

You've got to earn her trust

First.

Chipped watches

You can be whoever you want to be,

But

You're not cold-hearted.

You know damn well you have a heart.

Stop pretending you don't feel

Anything.

You feel everything

And there's nothing wrong with

Being sensitive.

Fake things and mean faces

Your words are as soft as your lips…

Pillows and feathers

Once I'm gone

Once you're gone

I'll find you all over again.

Might take me months,

May take me years.

I live to say I love you

Forever and more…

To the bitter end

Words are so important to women. Much more than you know. How you talk to her will either pull her close to you, or she'll resent all the hurtful things you've ever told her. So talk to her kindly, even if you don't feel like it. Tell her she's beautiful, even if she feels the opposite. Tell her she's smart, even if she thinks she's not. Tell her these things so she'll never forget.

Your words

With you,

My world is infinitely sweeter.

Water taste like lemonade

Air smells like lavender and honey

Clouds are cotton candy

Streets are dark chocolate.

I am a sugar fiend.

When you look at me

It's the topping on ice cream.

Sugar fiend

You'll meet whoever you are destined to meet

When you're ready to meet them.

In the meantime,

Make sure you love yourself.

Make sure you're whole.

Make sure you're so full of love

That your cup is spilling over.

Make sure you're healed.

Make sure you're happy.

In the meantime

This might seem strange to you

But your flaws

You think aren't attractive

Will be your most attractive trait

To someone else.

Your flaws

Side note:

If you tell her you love her,

And she says it back

For the first time,

She's loved you for a while now

And was waiting for you to

Say I love you first.

She does this because she's scared

Of putting herself out there

Without you holding her hand.

She's loved you

I've been hungry all day

And you're the only thing

I crave…

Dracula's fangs

Why do dangers and red flags make us want to know them more?

Teenage fantasy

We choose to be vulnerable

Because we crave intimacy,

Security,

And trust.

We give all these things away

Because we want to feel wanted.

So we share everything.

Here you go

She runs because

She's not ready to face

The monsters she's dated…

Bride of Frankenstein

It's not what they say,

It's how they treat you

That matters.

All that matters

If you fall for me

I promise to catch you.

Trust fall

If you wanna fight

Then we're going home…

Careful love

I'm sorry if I ever made you cry…

It's never too late

Too young

Too many temptations

Got in the way

Of being there

The way you wanted me to.

I played Russian roulette and

Gambled all your love away.

A bad hand

I went my own way

You followed

Hoping for better days.

I told myself never to look back

I couldn't stray.

I manned up

Outgrew old pains.

I still love you,

But not like

The old days.

Old days

Even if we fight

I'll hold you tight,

With all my might.

Tight

Appreciate people who chase after you. They see your worth and are attracted to it. They'll do whatever it takes to have an ounce of your time. They'll want to get to know you deeper than anyone else. They'll hang onto your every word. They'll support you. They'll plan trips because they want to see the world with you. They'll take all your free time because, for them, without you, time doesn't exist.

Chase after you

If I give you the stars and moon,

Will you give me the sun?

What will you give

You can't force someone to stay if they've decided to go. Their departure means they left the relationship long before they were brave enough to tell you they wanted to leave your life.

They already left

When you fell asleep in my arms,

I was ruined…

Ruined

When you cried,

I didn't cry with you because

I felt sorry for you,

I cried with you because

I wanted to feel everything you were feeling.

Felt

Hurting you the way you hurt me

Was an option.

But hurting you the way you hurt me

Wouldn't resolve anything.

I would have hated myself for seeping so low.

Hurt me hurt you

I traced your lips,

Your eyebrows,

Your freckles,

Your nose,

The shape of your almond eyes

To make sure you were real…

Really real

If you stare into my eyes for too long,

You'll get webbed in my deadly trap.

Traps

I asked you questions

That slowly opened you up.

I was dissecting your mind

Tying loose ends

Piecing together the real you

I was dying to meet.

The real you

We lounged in front of boring movies all day

Canceled reservations on rainy nights.

We agreed that

Conserving our body heat in bed was far more important.

Cuddles

I only went to the party because I knew you were there…

We've all done it

I would have flown to the sun

If you asked me to.

Burned by flames

Was the least of my concerns.

To the sun

Sharing the music playlist is the most sacred form of letting you in.

__Have you heard this song?__

If I can see a future with you,

That means I've sketched you into

The fabric of my life.

I can see where we'll live

I can see the vacations we'll go on

I can see myself telling you good morning

Every morning

For the rest of my life.

Future vision

Loyalty is rare.

Rare

If you miss me

Know that

I'll be

Where you can

Find me,

In your

Heart

Miss me

When the wind blows,

You won't have to worry about

Me floating away from you.

I'm too grounded.

Here to stay

To control her is like telling a bird not to fly too high…

Controlling

There are hands. Then there are your lovely hands

Hands

I thought I knew what a hug was

Until you wrapped your body

Around mine.

Your hugs made me feel my soul,

Reminded me to slow down

And enjoy the moment.

I replay those moments in my

Head all the time.

Small hugs

If you make her feel unimportant

She'll go out of her way

To find someone

Who thinks otherwise…

Unimportant

She's her most beautiful when she genuinely loves herself…

She is

We slept tangled in dewy fields.

Romance kept us warm.

Romance

I love you a thousand times more than infinity.

Time infinity

Dreams of you consume my head all night.

I much rather stay in bed

Where I can find you.

Dreaming of you

She only backs away to

Protect herself from

Being hurt again…

Eating alone

You don't have to be the best communicator.

You don't have to say much

When she needs you.

She'll appreciate you

For showing up

Because most people don't

Showing up

I followed you home

Because you were the only home

I knew…

Home struck

You can stand close to me.

I was going to stand close to you

Anyway.

Close to me

If you pour your heart out to me

I won't waste a single drop…

Pouring

If this was the end,

I would find a way to

Stretch today

To tomorrow to spend

A few more blissful hours

Adoring you…

End

She won't always need you

But she knows

You'll be there for her

When she does…

Need you

You don't grow to be sweet.

You're sweet

Because you taught yourself how.

Very sweet

If you're lost

Then I don't want to be found.

We can be undiscoverable together…

Together

An inch feels like a mile

A foot is yards

City to city

Is earth to mars

This is the disappointment

I go through

When our hands are so close

And do not touch

Earth to mars

Drunk on thoughts of you…

Red wine

She grows wherever she feels like growing…

Sunflower seeds

I knew I loved you

When I dared you to jump off a rock

And you jumped off a hill instead.

Wild child

If she's in your bubble

Then she wants you.

If she leans into the conversation

To talk to you,

She definitely wants you.

If she finds a way to touch your arm

When she laughs,

She wants you.

If she calls you past 10 p.m.

To tell you about her day,

She likes talking to you.

And she also wants you.

She wants you

Hugs are two hearts meeting.

I'm cutting onions that's why I'm crying

Don't overthink it and

Just call me when you miss me

Stand-by

My actions tell you how much I love you.

Actions

What's mine is mine.

I dare anyone

To take what I've built

With my two hands

And live in it.

A warm home

Isn't easy to make.

Home sweet home

When I think of you

I forget what gravity is…

Gravity

Kindness is one way to win her over.

Compassion is how you'll entice her.

Loyalty will keep her coming back.

Playfulness will pique her interest.

Patience will help her forgive you.

Her interest

Your smile is the most contagious disease.

Smile more

Why would I leave my most precious possession behind? Thieves are always ready to steal.

Possession

The moon always longs to be with the sun.

Longing

You were my pillow

And I was your blanket.

Pillows and blankets

Be as gentle as possible with her.

She won't tell you how

Breakable glass is.

Glass slipper

I hope you know that the pain they've caused you won't last forever. It hurts today because it's fresh. Know this: pain creates lessons. How badly they hurt you teaches you how you want to be treated. Let it hurt. Allow yourself to learn.

Let it hurt

She loves compliments, so give her lots.

Please and thank you

Lay roses at her feet when she walks.

She is a queen

Missing a crown.

Birthright

She's not quiet or shy.

She has excellent taste in people

And is careful who she lets in.

Knock first

Compromising never feels good.

Neglecting your needs feels worse.

Settling because you don't want to be alone

Leaves you empty.

A lifetime of regrets

Just a little lost in the snow

Melted wings

I forgot how to fly home

Where is home?

I think I asked

Before you left me here

In the cold.

I guess

I'm on my own

It's a little cold

Before I kiss you, tell me how much you love me…

Tell me

Her body is just a fraction of who she is. It's how lovely her soul is that should have you begging her for more.

Outer shell

I stare because I'm trying to capture every moment with you.

Photography

Listening to your heart

Is the only thing

That rocks me

To sleep.

Deep slumber

It's impossible to lift both sides of a beam.

If one side goes,

The foundation will be cricked and the roof

Ultimately

Caves in.

It takes two to build a house

Patiently waiting to love you for the rest of my life…

I'll wait here

I didn't know you

We just met

Yet

We couldn't stop laughing

When together

Where have you been?

Anything you buy

Is mine by default.

That's why I sample

Everything you order.

Let me have some

She knows when you're drifting away.

She feels the undoing of laces

Around her heart you knotted.

She feels the distance

Growing where she waters.

She waters too much

Trying to bring "us" back to life

Overwatering

It hurt when I pulled away and…you let go.

Tug of war

Laughing is a good sign.

You're in

You don't have to tell me when you're having a bad day. I can feel it.

Connected

When you know you're a catch,

You're not prone to jealousy.

When they talk to someone new

You're not worried.

All the temptations in the world

Doesn't mean anything to you.

If they leave you,

They're leaving the best love of their life

A love that would utterly consume them.

If you leave, it's okay

She will find ways to get closer to you if she's attracted to you. She'll sit next to you on the couch. She'll cross a busy dance floor to watch you move. She'll text you hello at midnight. She'll call off work to see you. She can't stop missing you.

I miss you

Don't wake me too soon

I want to dream of you for a few more minutes

Back to bed

We didn't need words

To talk.

Our eyes spoke

Languages

Only we

Understood.

Eyes

If you can't make me laugh, what's the point?

I'll be bored

All the little things I wish I said…

Up all night

If I could go back in time,

I would start with

The first time

I told you

Hello

My name is

I was the fool that waited for you after you left me…

Space gives her more time to miss you with.

Too much time

She needs her space.

Right in the middle is

Where you'll find her.

Ebb and flow

What is it about your skin?

I trace half crescent moons

So deliriously drunk

My fingers paint valleys

High and low.

It's how your breath catches

In your throat…

I sprawl

Lazily drawing

On your chest

Lazy painter

Your bad mood

Doesn't give you the right

To treat her any differently

Mood swings

One kiss will never be enough

One more

When we're together, time goes by so fast.

It's not fair.

Eight hours later

Me: we can't have everything in common

You: impresses me more

Me: (decided) we must be the same person

Too much in common

What you want is excitement and positive energy. You want to be surrounded by people who are excited to see you. Their energy will make you feel appreciated and wanted. They'll be great conversationalists, and you'll be their focal point.

Can I see you later?

What's important to her is how she feels and how you make her feel right now.

Her emotions are clever

I learned how to speak

Your love languages.

It was a priority.

To speak

If we're both yelling

I can't hear

How you really

Feel about it…

You go first

Lovely is the noticed daisy.

You're so beautiful

She takes everything you say to heart, so don't think you can get away with saying just anything. When you're gone, she'll play back your conversation. She won't tell you but will use your words against you. This is how she works.

Some advice

Don't worry.

If you go,

I'll leave the

Key under

The mat

For you

When

You

Come

Back

Home.

We'll

Talk

When

You

Feel

Better.

Porch lights on

She will test you from time to time.

It's nothing personal.

She's making sure

You're strong enough

To stay with her

Longer than

This unusually hot

Summer.

Lifetime warranty

Some days she might not like the shape of her waist. She might complain that her breasts aren't the way she likes. She might hate her fingernails. She might get annoyed with her frizzy hair. She might wish to change the body she has because there are too many things she dislikes. Tell her you love her thick waist. Tell her you like how her breasts feel on your chest. Tell her how perfect her fingernails feel when they scratch your skin. Tell her how frizzy hair makes her look exotic and wildly appetizing. Tell her how her body is made for you.

Ideal body

When she wants to talk, put your phone down and listen. This moment of vulnerability will fade if you neglect her presence. She's so intuitive that she'll stop opening up if she feels you're not paying attention.

I'm listening

So bad for me, but I'm sure we're addicted...

In confined

Spaces

With you

I lose

Control

Of my arms

And lips …

Lock the door

Lazy nights with you
I lounge in your arms…

Stays in

She kisses with her eyes closed

Thinking

How you'll

Reel her soul

Back

If she ever

Comes up

For air.

Deep breaths

Give her all the time she needs to decide if she wants you...

Go slow

She grows slowly.

The deeper her roots

The longer she'll stay

In your garden

Grows slowly

I've studied the stars,

And you're

More beautiful

No comparison

Intentionally ignores

Warning not to touch

Valuable art.

I teeter between ropes

And barriers.

A risk,

It certainly is.

Shall I break glass

To hold hands with

The statue of David again?

Statue of David

When you smile,

You radiate

In dark rooms

Not just a smile

I rest on your chest

Following all the lines

That shape your face

With my fingertips.

I see why mankind

Loves admiring art.

Lost looking at you

Daytime dreaming of you

My head underwater

Let me drown

The sea claims me.

Drowning

Thinking of you helps time pass by…

Two more hours

Where love is lost,

A heart is mending

In a place called alone.

Hearts must sew back together like this.

Mending heart

Be a skeptical lover.

Not eagerly waiting to fall in love quickly.

You are waiting for the best and

To find the best,

You have to weed out

The unprepared and immature

Before they know how

To make your heart

Skip beats.

Skeptical lover

She will have bad times.

Love her still.

Bad days

I loved you more than I hated your mistakes…

She reads your lips,

But your actions

She watches closely.

Looks with both eyes

Give energy when energy has been returned to you.
That's why your relationship feels so unbalanced.
You're the only one giving. They like your energy
but won't return it because they're too selfish.

Giving energy

Sometimes, we fall in love with who we wish they would be for us. That's why letting them go is so hard.

Read this again

It's not your job to figure out why someone doesn't want to love you right. You're not their therapist. All you need to know is that they don't want to love you the way you need to be loved and to move forward.

Overthinking the uncomplicated

A beautiful butterfly

Will land on the most

Enchanting flower

In the garden.

She looks for the best

If you treat her kindly,

She will be the most loving,

Compassionate,

Tender,

Romantic

Woman in the world.

Treat her kindly

Ignoring her is rude.

Grow up and text her back.

No one deserves to be left on read

Petty tings

If your love interest says, "I might hurt you."

Or

"I have trust issues."

Or

"It's hard for me to commit."

Those are red flags.

They're telling you that

There are things from their past

They haven't healed from

And will date you anyway.

What did you just say?

Tell me all your secrets

So I can keep them safe with me…

Treasure chest

They'll make it easy for you if they're interested in you. They won't randomly push you away, flake on dates, be mean or distant for no apparent reason, be hot and cold, play mind games… the list goes on.

Let your absence be their reward for not valuing you.

I'll be over here

You will lose

If you fight for someone

Who won't fight for you.

What are you fighting for again?

I'm sorry I wasn't as open as I could have been…

Too immature

I can't read your mind.
As close as we are.
It's better when you tell me
What's on your mind.
I don't want you to feel like
You have to carry the world
All by yourself.

What's really going on?

We met on earth

But we fell in love

Surrounded by stars.

Star crossed lovers

When she walks real close to you,

That's the okay

To hold her hand

Intentional bump

Be intentional with her. No mind tricks. No guessing games. If you want to take her on a date, tell her the time and place. Show her how straightforward you are. She hates it when she has to figure things out on her own. She'll get frustrated and feel out other propositions.

Tell her what you want

Being confident looks like leaving when you're not treated right and overlooked. You walk away. Your absence shows you mean business. You demand respect and are suddenly busy since you're not getting it.

Leave the party

If she doesn't feel close to you,
She'll say she doesn't know you.

We haven't gone deep yet

Give her space to fall in love with you.

Her emotions tell her everything

Growing up looks like walking away from one-sided relationships and no longer pouring into people who don't care if you come or go.

She's as lovely as a rose,

But don't get it twisted,

Hold her the wrong way

She'll prick your finger

Beast's rose

She only opens up to good people.

Her intuition has

Been sharpened to be

That good.

She's that good

She thinks closing herself off to keep from being hurt again is a good long term strategy…

She thought this through

I can feel you

From a million miles away.

Every thought you have of me

That's when I stop to think of you.

Miles away

She doesn't hate men

She hates how the men in her life

Treated her...

Patient and kind

Are two traits she wants

But are hard to find.

Rare diamonds

You'll overwhelm her if you pressure her into doing something. Her emotions guide her. She'll know what to do when her intuition tells her so.

Feel it in my soul

Give her what she wants,

A love that will envelop her whole

And leave nothing but her heart aching for more.

Passion that rips her apart and

Sets her world on fire.

She wants adventure and fun

A smidge of cool and goofy to cheer her up.

She wants thrill to wake her up

And smoldering heat to entice her body.

She wants what we all want

Give her what she wants

If you cry a thousand storms

I will count each raindrop

Every tear

I will wipe away.

A thousand storms

We fought

We argued

And I will still come home to you.

Homebound

If I kiss you,

You're stuck with me.

The kiss of death

She'll like you more if you learn how to listen to her when she speaks. She hates being interrupted.

Listen first

Jealousy isn't birthed out of thin air…

Mistakes

When you need me, I'll be right here.

A phone call away

When she least expects it,

Ask her how her day was.

Look at her

Like she has all the time in the world

To answer.

She'll love that.

Tell me everything

Wherever you dig
Water will surely flow

Shovel and pail

My every bone is romantic…

Swept off feet

Give me your love,

You have my trust

Trust fall

Thinking of you is far too dangerous for the average human…

Too dangerous

She kisses like a savage

And thinks like an evil genius.

She's too hot to handle

Be very afraid of her

I have no idea where I go when we lock eyes.

I just know

I'm no longer home in my body.

Out of body

If being apart from me is too hard,
Come closer.

Come close

I didn't fall in love with you. I collided.

Crash

Her vulnerability is thoughtfully given.

She gives because she knows

You'll keep it safe.

Tell me your story

I know you're tough and strong

But you don't have to carry it all alone on

Your back.

When you're weak

I will be strong for you

And when I'm weak

You can be strong for me.

Let me carry your burdens.

Rest.

Use me to wipe all your tears away.

A kind and balanced relationship

Be with someone who truly loves you.

You don't have to tone down to fit in beside them.

You can be as loud and as crazy as you are.

You don't have to pretend to like something

You can hate and they'll back you up

You don't have to hide your ideas and dreams

They'll help you pull out all your creativity

And more.

They'll accept all of you,

Your flaws,

The weird memes you love

Your funny quirks

Your passions

Your drive

Your scars

It all

I love all of you and everything in between

I treated you the same…even after you hurt me

You're a little weird

And that's okay.

I'm attracted to your little weird.

So you're addicted to avocados?

You can be both vulnerable and strong.

You can

A star can choose to shine alone.

But it doesn't have to.

I am the star next to you.

We can shine together

Neighboring stars

I see how beautiful your heart is.

Inner mirror

Kindness brought out the best of her.

Hurt brought out the worst in her.

Treat her kindly

She is lovely…

To those who make her feel loved.

She has two sides

She will never leave if you create an environment where she feels safe, comfortable, heard, appreciated, loved, and adored.

Build this home with your hands

Open the gates to your heart

I offer only peace

Friendship

Loyalty

And good humor

To lighten this dreary atmosphere

Trojan horse

With me

You can dream of flying

And I'll make you wings

Fly with support

Feet dig deeper

The more you

Water my soul…

Watering

We can fly to the moon together.

Above

So jealous

Of night

How it takes

The light

From your eyes

In spite of the

Heights you take my heart

Oh

It delights

Fears emerge without light

Please hold her tight

With all your might

She no longer frights

When cradled just right

Nighttime poem

Toxic people never realize

How toxic they are.

A kiss on your rib.

Wishbone

Smile for me

It's all I need.

Smile for me

Battling this world

Come home to me

I will

Wash all your

Bloody scars

Fresh scars

When you dropped me

It shouldn't have surprised you

That I broke…

Shattered plates

Sensitive souls love the hardest.

Sensitive souls

You're not over it

Until it no longer hurts

Scabs

Souls never disconnect

They just try their best

To live apart.

Disconnection

If you kiss me goodbye,

I'll end up wanting another more…

Another one, please

Words are so important to women, much more than you know. How you speak to her will either pull her close to you, or she'll resent all the hurtful things you told her. So talk to her kindly, even if you don't feel like it. Tell her she's beautiful when she feels the opposite. Tell her she's smart when she thinks she's not. Remind her of these things.

Kind words

There's no room for hate, only love.

A born lover

Set on fire, flames no longer burn me.

Fire walker

I love all my scars,

Even the healing,

Bloody ones still closing.

Bloody knees

When told she's important and seen,

She floats mid-air…

She can fly

When we're treated like s**t

We forget who we are.

Once we realize we are the s**t

We stop letting people who

Aren't worth s**t tear us down.

I'm the s**t

If you can control your moods

You'll be in control of your destiny…

Remain cool

If you keep looking at me like that

I'm going to have to

Do something about it…

That's a threat

If I wasn't in love

I wouldn't have fought so hard

To keep you…

Fought my hardest

You made it to the end! Now it's time to leave a review! Share your thoughts with the world.

Thank you!

About the author

Ry Reed has written poetry for many years. Poetry has helped her heal, and she uses her life as a platform to teach and share lessons she's learned along her journey. Depression, heartbreak, and willingness to move forward and start over again, her poems are relatable, personal, and straight to the point. Her every word digs out emotions and encourages change. She lives in southern California with her mother and brothers and writes poetry, non-fiction, and fiction books.

WALKING ON THE MOON

WALKING ON THE MOON. *Copyright* © 2021 by Kelli Ry Reed. All rights reserved, including the right to reproduce, distribute, or transmit in any form or means. For information regarding subsidiary rights, please get in touch with the author.

This is a work of fiction/poetry. Names, characters, places, and incidents are products of the author's imagination or used fictitiously, and any resemblance to persons, living or dead, actual events, or locales is coincidental.

ISBN: 978-0-9981459-4-5

ISBN eBook: 978-0-9981459-5-2

https://ryreedthewriter.com/

Subjects: Poetry/ Love / Romance/ Relationships

Summary: Falling in love feels like floating. Gravity loosens its ties on your feet, and you fly. Everything that makes sense is illogical. You find yourself rushing towards a feeling, a pull you can't quite explain, but you love how light you feel, where you're going, and you're okay with not looking back down at earth for reassurance. Ry Reed's WALKING ON THE MOON is romantic bliss—a timeless tale about falling hopelessly in love.

Latest Releases

Ry Reed

A WELL OF THOUGHTS

Pink Grapefruit

Ry Reed

White Orchids

Ry Reed

Ry Reed's social media

INSTAGRAM: @ry.reed.the.writer

PINTEREST: Ry Reed the writer

YOUTUBE: Ry Reed the Writer

FACEBOOK: ryreedauthorandpoet

WEBSITE: https://ryreedthewriter.com/

Manufactured by Amazon.ca
Acheson, AB